Some folks may think I'm just a pet,
They haven't gotten to know me yet.

I'm a reliable friend and a comfort, too.
Sometimes I think I'm just like you.

This is a scrapbook we can share,
It shows how much you really care.

I know you'll like it, and you'll see
we share a lot of fond memories

Gather those pictures of cute things I do.
Be as proud of me as I am of you.

Created by Susan and Kerry Kelley,
with contributions by Lindsay and Erin Kelley

Susan Kelley Pet Diaries
Richmond, Virginia
www.petphotodiary.com
ISBN 0-9771624-1-9

Paste your kitty picture here

Hi there!

My name is _____

This book is
all about me!!

MY BABY PICTURE

My hair color is _____

My eyes are _____

I am a _____ boy _____ girl

I am

_____ a registered purebred

_____ simply a proud mix

My birthday is _____

I was born here _____

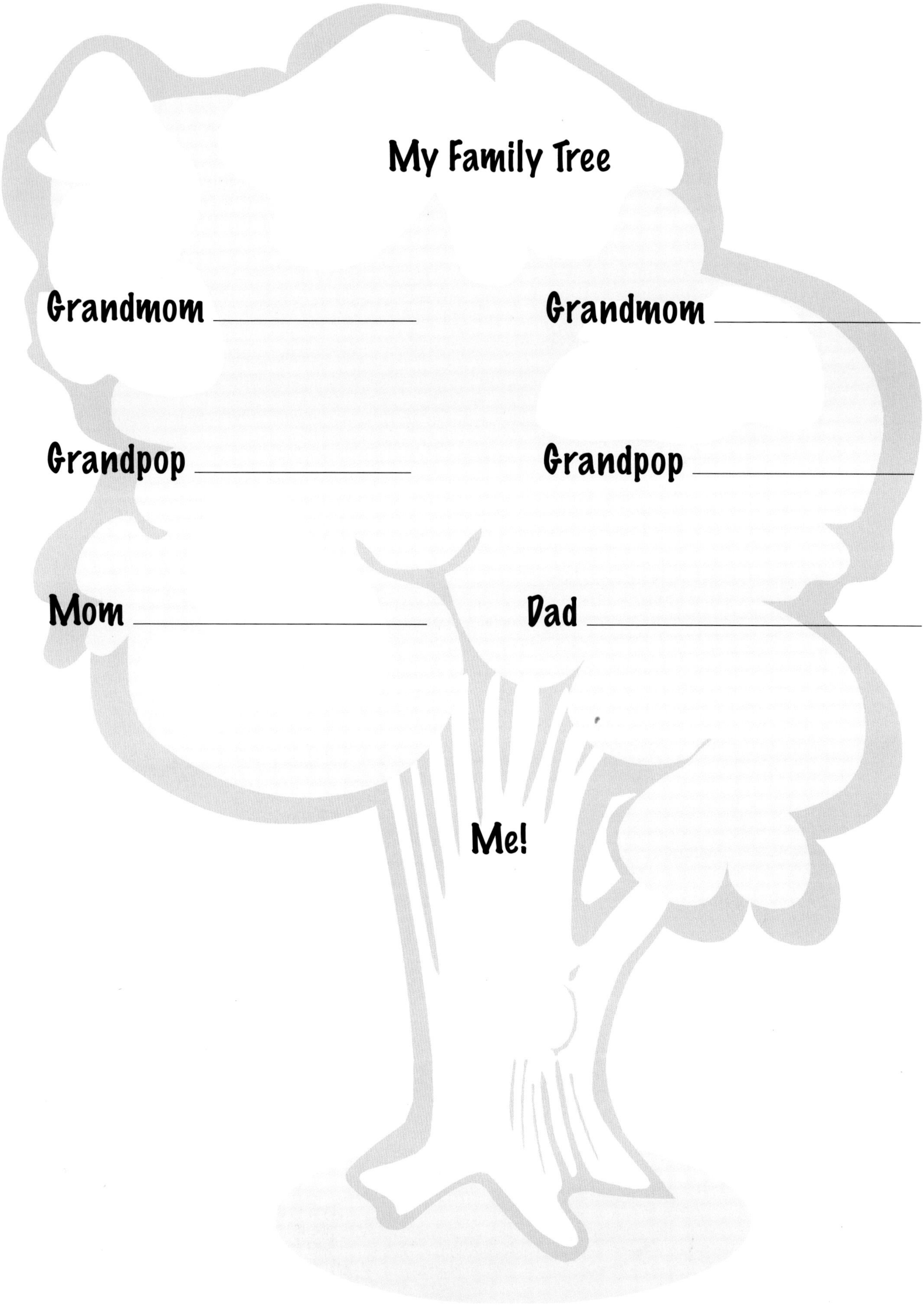

My Family Tree

Grandmom _____

Grandmom _____

Grandpop _____

Grandpop _____

Mom _____

Dad _____

Me!

I was a cuddly kitten.

Snapshots

More cuddly pictures.

Snapshots

Snapshots

My visits to the vet.

Vet's Name: _____

Address: _____

Phone: _____

Fears I may have: _____

Well, nobody likes shots!

Medical records

visit _____

reason _____

visit _____

reason _____

visit _____

reason _____

visit _____

reason _____

visit _____

reason _____

Did I need any surgeries?

Better make some notes...

_____

_____

_____

_____

_____

_____

_____

_____

_____

Was I a good patient?

Snapshots

Or did I mope?

Snapshots

This is my proud new family,

Snapshots

and cute pictures they took of me.

Snapshots

These are things I like to do

Sometimes alone, sometimes with you.

These are my brand new relatives...

Snapshots

and some of my very close friends . .

Snapshots

Birthdays and Holidays. . .

Snapshots

Lazy and sunny days

Snapshots

Mischievous cat

Snapshots

Caught in the act.

Snapshots

Snuggly spaces. .

Snapshots

hiding places. . .

Snapshots

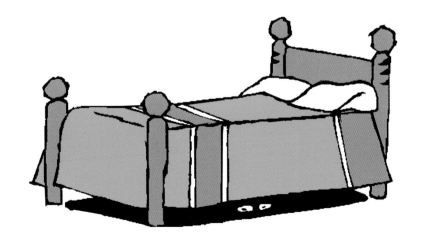

I like my ears scratched...

Snapshots

and my back being rubbed. . .

Snapshots

But the best thing in
<u>My</u> world. . .

Snapshots

is just to be loved.

Thanks for loving me!